FOOD LOVERS

COOKING FOR
CHILDREN

RECIPES SELECTED BY JONNIE LÉGER

Trans
Atlantic
Press

All recipes serve four people, unless otherwise indicated.

For best results when cooking the recipes in this book, buy fresh ingredients and follow the instructions carefully. Make sure that everything is properly cooked through before serving, particularly any meat and shellfish, and note that as a general rule vulnerable groups such as the very young, elderly people, pregnant women, convalescents and anyone suffering from an illness should avoid dishes that contain raw or lightly cooked eggs.

For all recipes, quantities are given in standard U.S. cups and imperial measures, followed by the metric equivalent. Follow one set or the other, but not a mixture of both because conversions may not be exact. Standard spoon and cup measurements are level and are based on the following:

1 tsp. = 5 ml, 1 tbsp. = 15 ml, 1 cup = 250 ml / 8 fl oz.

Note that Australian standard tablespoons are 20 ml, so Australian readers should use 3 tsp. in place of 1 tbsp. when measuring small quantities.

The electric oven temperatures in this book are given for conventional ovens with top and bottom heat. When using a fan oven, the temperature should be decreased by about 20–40°F / 10–20°C – check the oven manufacturer's instruction book for further guidance. The cooking times given should be used as an approximate guideline only.

CONTENTS

DICED SALMON WITH SOY DIP

Ingredients

1 lb 2 oz / 500 g salmon fillets, without skin, cut into bite-size cubes

For the marinade:

2 lemons, juice and zest

1 tbsp. whole grain mustard

1 tbsp. olive oil

For the dip:

1 red chili

1 scallion (spring onion)

5 tbsp. light soy sauce

1 tbsp. chopped cilantro (coriander) leaves

Method

Prep and cook time: 20 min plus marinating time 30 min

1 Mix together all ingredients for the marinade and marinate the salmon cubes for about 30 minutes.

2 Remove the salmon from the marinade and place under a hot broiler (grill) for 2–3 minutes until lightly browned. Brush with marinade from time to time.

3 For the dip, wash, de-seed and finely chop the chili. Wash and trim the scallion (spring onion) and cut into rings.

4 Mix all the dip ingredients and season to taste. Serve the salmon with the dip.

SPAGHETTI WITH MEATBALLS AND TOMATO SAUCE

Ingredients

12 oz / 350 g spaghetti

For the meatballs:

1 slice stale white bread

3 tbsp. cream

14 oz / 400 g ground (minced) beef

1 egg

2 tbsp. chopped fresh parsley

Lemon zest, finely chopped

Salt & freshly milled pepper

Butter

For the tomato sauce:

1 clove garlic

2 shallots

4 tbsp. olive oil

1 tsp. tomato paste (purée)

14 oz / 400 g can chopped tomatoes

Salt & freshly milled pepper

½ tsp. sugar

Fresh parsley, to garnish

Method

Prep and cook time: 40 min

1 For the meatballs, roughly chop the bread and soak it in cream until soft. Squeeze the bread to remove excess cream, and then mix together with the ground (minced) beef, egg, chopped parsley and lemon zest. Season with salt and pepper and mix well. Form small balls from the mix.

2 For the tomato sauce, peel and finely chop the garlic and the shallots. Fry in hot olive oil in a saucepan until soft. Stir in the tomato paste (purée), followed by the chopped tomatoes. Simmer gently for about 20 minutes. Season with salt, pepper and sugar.

3 Cook the spaghetti in boiling, salted water according to instructions on the packet.

4 Fry the meatballs in butter for 6–8 minutes on all sides. Drain the spaghetti and divide onto plates, arrange the meatballs on the top and spoon some of the tomato sauce over everything. Garnish with parsley and serve.

FRIED HAM AND CHEESE SANDWICHES

Ingredients

3 eggs

2/3 cup / 150 ml milk

3 tbsp. butter

8 slices white sandwich bread

Parsley leaves

4 slices ham

4 slices cheese

Method

Prep and cook time: 30 min

1 Whisk the eggs with the milk.

2 Heat the butter in a skillet. Dip the slices of bread briefly in the egg and milk mixture and fry on both sides in butter over a medium heat, until golden brown.

3 Lay a parsley leaf on four of the slices of bread, and then add a slice of ham and a slice of cheese. Put under a hot broiler (grill) until the cheese has melted.

4 Put the other four slices of bread on top, halve the sandwiches diagonally and serve at once.

MEATBALL SPIDERS

Ingredients

For the meatballs:

1 stale bread roll

1 onion

Oil for frying

1 bay leaf

1 lb 6 oz / 600 g mixed ground meat

1 egg

1 tsp mustard

1 tbsp. chopped parsley

Salt & freshly milled pepper

To decorate:

Strips of red and green bell pepper

Mayonnaise

Capers

Method

Prep and cook time: 25 min

1 Roughly chop the bread roll and soak it in warm water.

2 Chop the onion. Heat the oil in a skillet and gently fry the chopped onion and bay leaf until the onion is soft but not browned.

3 Remove the bay leaf and mix the onion with the squeezed-out bread roll, ground meat, egg, mustard, parsley, salt and pepper.

4 Mix well. Using wet hands, form into small meatballs and fry gently on all sides in oil until cooked (about 10 minutes).

5 To serve, arrange the meatballs on plates. Attach strips of bell pepper to form 'spider's legs' make eyes from dabs of mayonnaise and capers and a mouth from a triangle of bell pepper attached with mayonnaise.

TOMATO SOUP WITH CROUTONS

Ingredients

1 large carrot

2 tbsp. olive oil

1 shallot

1 tsp. flour

14 oz / 400 g can of tomatoes, diced

2½ cups / 600 ml vegetable broth (stock)

2 thick slices white bread

2–3 tbsp. grated cheese, such as Cheddar or Gouda

Salt

1–2 pinches sugar

Method

Prep and cook time: 40 min

1 Finely dice the carrot and the shallot. Heat 1 tablespoon of the oil and sauté the diced carrot and shallot. Add the flour and cook briefly. Add the tomatoes and vegetable broth (stock), cover and simmer for about 20 minutes.

2 Pre-heat the oven to 350°F (180°C / Gas Mark 4). For the croutons, cut the crusts off the bread, cut the bread into cubes and put on a cookie sheet. Sprinkle with the rest of the oil and bake in the oven for 8–10 minutes, until golden brown. Sprinkle with grated cheese and bake for a further 2 minutes.

3 Purée the soup, season with salt and add sugar to taste. Ladle into bowls and serve garnished with croutons.

PIZZA PANCAKES

Ingredients

For the pancake batter:

3 cups / 300 g all-purpose (plain) flour

1¼ cups / 300 ml milk

3 eggs

1/3–½ cup / 100 ml sparkling water

¼ cup / 50 g whipping cream

1 tsp. salt

1 tbsp. pizza seasoning (optional)

3 tbsp. oil

For the topping:

¼ cup / 40 g Parmesan, grated

½ cup / 60 g Emmental cheese, grated

4 oz / 100 g salami, thinly sliced

2 red bell peppers

Method

Prep and cook time: 30 min plus standing time 30 min

1 Mix the flour and milk smoothly, add the rest of the pancake batter ingredients and beat to a smooth batter. Leave to stand for 30 minutes.

2 Meanwhile, wash, halve, core and dice the red bell peppers.

3 Heat a little oil in a skillet and make thin pancakes one after the other over a medium heat.

4 When the first side of each pancake is cooked turn the pancake, sprinkle with a little cheese and top with salami and diced bell pepper. Add a little more cheese, and then put a lid on the skillet for 1 minute, until the cheese has melted (or put the skillet under a broiler (grill) to melt the cheese).

5 When done keep the pizza pancakes warm in the oven while you make more pancakes with the rest of the batter.

ONION BHAJIS

Ingredients

2 onions

2 green chilis

½ tsp. chili powder

2 tbsp. finely chopped cilantro
(coriander) leaves

3 tbsp. lemon juice

1 tsp. cumin seeds, roughly crushed in
a mortar

7 tbsp. chickpea flour (gram flour)

Pinch of salt

2 tbsp. water

2 cups / 500 ml sunflower oil, for
deep-frying

Method
Prep and cook time: 40 min

1 Peel the onions and slice into very thin rings.
Wash the chilis, slit open lengthways, remove the
seeds and white inner ribs and finely dice the flesh.
Mix both with the chili powder, cilantro (coriander),
lemon juice and cumin.

2 Stir the chickpea flour and salt into the onion
mixture. Add the water and mix well.

3 Heat the oil in a pan (it is hot enough when
bubbles form on the handle of a wooden spoon held
in the oil). Take small balls of the onion mixture with
a teaspoon and fry in the hot oil, a few at a time,
until golden. Drain on a paper towel and keep warm
in the oven at the lowest heat. When all the bhajis
are cooked, serve at once.

MINI PIZZAS

Ingredients

For 12 mini pizzas

For the pizza base:

4 cups / 400 g all-purpose (plain) flour

¾ oz / 20 g dried yeast

1 tsp. sugar

1 tsp. salt

1 cup /240 ml lukewarm water

For the pizza topping:

5 tbsp. olive oil

3 cups / 600 g tomato sauce (passata)

Salt and freshly milled pepper

4 oz / 100 g dried tomatoes in oil, drained and chopped

¼ cup / 50 g green olives, pitted and chopped

1²/3 cup / 200 g grated cheese

2 bunches of rocket leaves, to garnish

2 tbsp. lemon juice

Method

Prep and cook time: 45 min plus raising time 1 h 40 min

1 For the pizza base, mix together the flour, yeast, sugar, salt and the lukewarm water. Knead to form a smooth dough, then cover and put in a warm place for about 1 hour to rise. Knead the dough again, cover and leave for 30–40 minutes to rise again.

2 Line a cookie sheet with parchment paper. Divide the pizza dough into 12 balls. Roll out each ball on a floured surface. Place on the cookie sheet and press flat, leaving the edge slightly thicker.

3 Pre-heat the oven to 425°F (220°C / Gas Mark 7). Brush each pizza base with a little of the olive oil, then spread tomato sauce (passata) over the top. Season with salt and pepper.

4 Chop the well-drained, dried tomatoes and scatter over the mini-pizzas, together with the chopped olives. Now sprinkle the grated cheese over the top and bake in the oven for about 8–12 minutes until golden brown.

5 Wash the rocket leaves. Mix the lemon juice and 3 tablespoons olive oil and season with salt. Toss the rocket leaves in the oil and lemon dressing. Arrange the mini-pizzas around the rocket salad and serve.

BAKED POTATOES WITH CHEESE AND BACON TOPPING

Ingredients

For the potatoes:

10 medium-sized baking potatoes

2 tbsp. olive oil

Salt & freshly milled pepper

20 slices bacon

20 slices cheese

1 cup lamb's lettuce, to garnish

For the chive cheese dip:

1 cup / 250 g cream cheese

1²/₃ cup / 400 ml sour cream

½ tsp. vegetable broth (stock) granules

Salt

Ground white pepper

2–4 tbsp. fresh chives, chopped

Method

Prep and cook time: 45 min

1 Pre-heat the oven at 400°F (200°C / Gas Mark 6). Wash the potatoes well, and then cut in half lengthways. Brush a roasting pan with olive oil and place the potatoes on the roasting pan, cut side downwards. Bake in the oven for about 25 minutes.

2 In the meantime, mix together all ingredients for the cheese dip, reserving 1 tablespoon of chopped chives for the garnish. Season to taste with salt and pepper, then spoon into a bowl and garnish with chives.

3 When the potatoes are cooked, remove from the oven. Heat the broiler (grill) to 475°F (250°C).

4 Carefully take the potatoes off the roasting pan and season the flat side with salt and pepper. Place the bacon on the top of the potato and cover with cheese. Place under the broiler until golden brown. Serve the potatoes on a plate, together with the cheese dip. Garnish with a few leaves of lamb's lettuce.

CHICKEN NUGGETS

Ingredients

1 lb 6 oz / 600 g chicken breast

Salt & freshly milled pepper

3–4 tbsp. all-purpose (plain) flour

2 eggs

2 cups breadcrumbs, to coat

Fat for frying

Chili sauce or tomato ketchup

Method
Prep and cook time: 30 min

1 Wash the chicken breasts and pat dry. Cut into bite-size pieces and season with salt and pepper.

2 Lightly coat the chicken pieces with flour. Whisk the eggs in a bowl. Place the breadcrumbs on a plate. Coat the chicken pieces with egg, then roll in the breadcrumbs and press down well.

3 Fry the nuggets in hot fat for 3–4 minutes until the chicken is cooked. Drain on a paper towel. Serve with chili sauce or tomato ketchup.

PIZZA PINWHEELS

Ingredients

Makes 12

14 oz / 400 g puff pastry, defrosted

1 onion

1 clove garlic

2 bell peppers, yellow and red

2 tbsp. olive oil

2 tbsp. chopped fresh parsley

1 tsp. dried oregano

2 balls mozzarella, diced

4 tbsp. Parmesan cheese, grated

Salt

Freshly milled pepper

¾ cup / 150 g tomato sauce (passata)

Method

Prep and cook time: 1 h

1 Pre-heat the oven to 400°F (200°C / Gas Mark 6).

2 Peel and finely chop the onion and the garlic. Wash, halve, de-seed and finely chop the bell peppers.

3 Sauté the pepper together with the onions and garlic in hot oil for about 5 minutes so that all liquid has evaporated. Stir continually. Remove from the heat and let cool. Mix in the herbs and the cheese and season with salt and pepper.

4 Roll out the puff pastry to a rectangle 12 x 8 inches (35 x 20 cm). Spread the tomato sauce (passata) over the puff pastry, leaving a 1-inch (2-cm) wide edge free all the way round.

5 Spread the bell pepper filling over the top. Wet the edge of the puff pastry with a little water and roll up, pressing the edge down firmly. Cut 12 slices (pinwheels) and place them on a cookie sheet lined with parchment paper.

6 Bake in the oven for about 20–25 minutes until golden brown.

LENTIL BURGERS WITH YOGURT DIP

Ingredients

1 cup / 200 g brown lentils

Some fresh thyme

1 bay leaf

1 stale wholegrain bread roll

1 onion

2 cloves garlic

3 tbsp. sunflower oil

1 bunch parsley

1 chili

1 carrot

2 tbsp. sesame seeds

Pinch ground cumin

Pinch ground coriander

Pinch ground nutmeg

Pinch cayenne pepper

1 egg

2 tbsp. flour

For the yoghurt dip:

2 scallions (spring onions)

1 cup / 200 g plain yoghurt

Salt

Method

Prep and cook time: 1 h 20 min

1 Rinse the lentils under running, cold water, then place in a large pan together with 4 cups (1 litre) of water, the thyme and bay leaf. Cover with a lid and cook for about 30–35 minutes until soft.

2 During the last 5 minutes of cooking, open the lid and cook on a high heat, stirring constantly until all the liquid has evaporated and the lentils are beginning to fall into pieces. Remove the thyme and the bay leaf.

3 Soak the bread in warm water. Peel and finely chop the onion and the garlic. Fry in 1 tablespoon of oil until golden, then season with salt.

4 Finely chop the parsley leaves. Add the chopped parsley to the onions and remove from the heat. Wash, halve, de-seed and finely chop the chili. Peel and grate the carrot. Squeeze the water out of the bread roll.

5 Mix the lentils with the chopped chili, salt, onion mix, bread, carrots, sesame seeds and spices and season to taste. Add the egg and the flour and form 8 flat patties. Brush with the remaining oil and fry gently for about 5 minutes on each side.

6 For the yogurt dip, wash and trim the scallions (spring onions) and cut into thin rings. Mix with the yogurt and season to taste with salt. Serve the burgers with the yogurt dip and salad.

LASAGNE

Ingredients

7 oz / 200 g lasagne sheets (no pre-cook type)

For the Bolognese sauce:

1 onion

2 cloves garlic

1 carrot

3 stalks celery

3 tbsp. olive oil

8 oz / 250 g mixed pork and beef ground (minced) meat

2 tbsp. tomato paste (purée)

¼ cup / 50 ml red wine

14 oz / 400 g can chopped tomatoes

Salt

Freshly milled pepper

2/3 cup / 80g Parmesan cheese, freshly grated

5oz / 150 g mozzarella

For the béchamel sauce:

4 tbsp. / 60 g butter

3–4 tbps. / 50 g all-purpose (plain) flour

2 cups / 500 ml milk

Method

Prep and cook time: 1 h 45 min

1 Peel the onion and the garlic and finely chop. Peel and trim the carrot and the celery and finely chop. Cut the mozzarella into thin slices.

2 Heat the olive oil in a skillet and fry the onions, garlic and ground meat. Add the carrots and the celery and sauté. Stir in the tomato paste (purée) and pour in the red wine and chopped tomatoes. Season with salt and pepper, and then simmer for about 20 minutes.

3 For the béchamel sauce, melt 3½ tbsp. (50 g) of the butter in a pan. Stir in the flour and cook over a low heat. Gradually add the milk, stirring continually, and then season to taste with salt and pepper. Simmer gently for 5 minutes, stirring continually.

4 Pre-heat the oven to 400°F (200°C / Gas Mark 6).

5 Spoon 2–3 tablespoons of béchamel sauce into a baking dish. Place a layer of lasagne sheets on top, followed by a layer of the Bolognese sauce. Repeat the process, and then finish with a layer of lasagne sheets and top with the remaining béchamel sauce. Cover the top with a layer of mozzarella slices and grated Parmesan cheese. Put a few knobs of butter on the top and then bake in the oven for about 40 minutes until cooked.

MINI HAMBURGERS

Ingredients
Makes 12

14 oz / 400 g ground beef

Salt & pepper to taste

Oil to fry

12 mini hamburger buns

4 tbsp. tomato ketchup

3 tomatoes

1 handful cress

In addtion:
Some colored toothpicks

Method
Prep and cook time: 30 min

1 Mix the ground beef with salt and pepper and form into 12 small patties.

2 Heat the oil in a skillet and fry the hamburgers on both sides for 3–4 minutes, a few at a time.

3 Cut the hamburger buns in half and spread some tomato ketchup on the bottom half.

4 Slice the tomatoes. Place a hamburger pattie on the lower half of the bun, followed by a slice of tomato and some cress. Finish with the top half of the bun and secure with a toothpick.

GRILLED CHICKEN WITH DIP

Ingredients

16 chicken wings

For the marinade:

Few dashes Tabasco sauce

4 tbsp. oil

1 tbsp. honey

1 tbsp. ketchup

2 tbsp. chili sauce

1 tbsp. vinegar

Salt & freshly milled pepper

1 scallion (spring onion), finely chopped

For the mango dip:

1 mango

1 tbsp. honey

1 tbsp. rosemary leaves

Lime juice, to taste

Method

Prep and cook time: 45 min plus marinating time 12 h

1 For the marinade, mix the Tabasco sauce, oil, honey, ketchup, chili sauce and vinegar. Season well with salt and pepper and stir in the scallions (spring onions).

2 Wash and dry the chicken pieces and brush with the marinade. Cover and marinate, preferably overnight. Then cook on a grill over a medium heat for 15–20 minutes, turning frequently.

3 For the mango dip, finely purée the flesh of a mango with 1 tablespoon honey and 1 tablespoon rosemary leaves. Add a little lime juice to taste.

4 Serve the chicken wings with a separate dish of mango dip.

RASPBERRY YOGURT ICE CREAM

Ingredients

1 lb 2 oz / 500 g raspberries

Generous ¾ cup /200 g natural yogurt

1–1½ cup / 125–200 g confectioner's (icing) sugar, to taste

2 tbsp. lemon juice

2 cups / 500 ml whipping cream

Method

Prep and cook time: 40 min plus freezing time 4 h

1 Wash the raspberries then drain well. Purée the raspberries with the yogurt and the lemon juice and add sugar to taste.

2 Fold about ½ cup (125 ml) of the cream into about ⅓ of the raspberry purée.

3 Mix the remaining cream with the rest of the raspberry purée. Pour the lighter raspberry cream into 6–8 clean yogurt cups. Place in the freezer for about 30 minutes.

4 Remove the cups from the freezer and put a wooden stick in each. Pour in the remaining raspberry cream. Freeze for about 3–4 hours.

5 Shortly before serving, place the yogurt cups into hot water, and then carefully push the ice cream out of the yogurt cup onto on a plate. Serve immediately.

MINI CHOCOLATE CUPCAKES

Ingredients

For a 24-hole cupcake pan

For the cake batter:

3–4 oz / 100 g dried plums, pitted

Scant ¼ cup / 50 ml apple juice

1 egg

3 tbsp. /50 g soft butter

½ cup / 100 g sugar

Pinch salt

1 tsp. vanilla extract

4 oz / 125 g milk chocolate
(30% cocoa solids)

½ cup / 125 ml milk

1¼ cups / 125 g all-purpose
(plain) flour

1 tsp. baking powder

For the decoration:

8 oz / 250 g bittersweet (plain)
cooking chocolate (70% cocoa solids)

Colorful chocolate beans

Method

Prep and cook time: 1 h 15 min

1 Chop the plums, then mix with the apple juice and let soak. Separate the egg. Beat the egg yolk, butter, ¼ cup / 40 g of the sugar, salt and vanilla extract until smooth and creamy. Break the chocolate into pieces and melt in a bowl over a pan of hot water. Stir into the egg mix, and then slowly add the milk and the plums. Add the flour and the baking powder. Whisk the egg white with the remaining sugar until stiff and fold into the cake batter.

2 Pre-heat the oven to 350°F (180°C / Gas Mark 4). Line the holes of the cupcake pan with baking cups and pour in the cake batter, just about filling each cup. Bake in the oven for about 25 minutes. Let cool in the cupcake tin for 5 minutes, then remove and place on a wire rack to cool completely.

3 Melt the cooking chocolate. Drizzle a little chocolate over the cupcakes and decorate with chocolate beans.

JAM TARTS

Ingredients

For a 12-hole tartlet pan

1¾ cups / 175 g all-purpose
(plain) flour

⅓ cup / 85 g butter

6 tbsp. cold water

¾ cup / 250 g conserve or jelly (jam)
of your choice

Flour for working

Butter for the tartlet pan

Method

Prep and cook time: 45 min

1 Preheat the oven to 400°F (200°C / Gas Mark 6).

2 Butter and chill the tartlet pan.

3 Rub the butter into the flour until it resembles breadcrumbs, then add the water and work to a pliable dough. Roll out on a floured work surface and cut out circles a little bigger than the holes in the tartlet pan.

4 Press the pastry circles into the holes and fill each with about 1 tablespoon of conserve or jelly (jam). Cut hearts, stars or other shapes out of the pastry scraps and put one on top of each jam tart.

5 Bake the tarts in the oven for about 15 minutes. Take out of the oven, leave in the pan for short while and then take out and cool on a cake rack.

CHOCOLATE GLAZED STRAWBERRIES

Ingredients

1 lb 2 oz / 500 g fresh strawberries

5 oz / 150 g bittersweet (plain) cooking chocolate (70% cocoa solids)

5 oz / 150 g white cooking chocolate

¾ cup / 75 g colored sugar sprinkles

¾ cup / 75 g hazelnuts, roasted and chopped

Method

Prep and cook time: 30 min

1 Wash the strawberries carefully, leaving stems and leaves intact, then pat dry. Chop the dark chocolate and white chocolate into small pieces and melt in separate bowls over two pans of hot water.

2 Put the chopped hazelnuts and the sugar sprinkles in separate bowls.

3 Dip half of the strawberries in the white chocolate and the remaining strawberries in the dark chocolate. Place some on a wire rack to dry and dip the others in the chopped hazelnuts or the sugar sprinkles.

4 Make two paper cones out of parchment paper and fill each with different chocolate (or put the chocolate into freezer bags and cut off a corner to make a tiny hole).

5 Cut the end off the paper cone and drizzle the white chocolate over the remaining dark chocolate strawberries, the dark chocolate over the remaining white chocolate strawberries.

BLUEBERRY PANCAKES WITH MAPLE SYRUP

Ingredients

For the pancakes:

2 eggs

2 cups / 200 g all-purpose (plain) flour

2½ tsp. baking powder

Pinch of salt

1¼ cups / 300 ml milk

2 tbsp. clear honey

2 cups / 200 g blueberries

Butter for frying

For the topping:

Maple syrup

Method

Prep and cook time: 20 min plus standing time 30 min

1 Separate the eggs and beat the egg whites until stiff. Put the rest of the ingredients, apart from the blueberries and butter, into a mixing bowl and beat with an electric mixer to produce a smooth batter. Let the batter rest for 30 minutes

2 Wash and drain the blueberries and fold into the pancake batter with the beaten egg whites.

3 To make the pancakes, heat a little butter in a skillet, add a spoonful of pancake batter and spread out to a circle approximately 4–5 inches (12 cm) in diameter. Fry for 2–3 minutes on one side, then turn and cook the other side. Take out of the pan and keep warm. Continue making pancakes in this way until all the batter is used up.

4 Pile the pancakes on plates, drizzle with maple syrup and serve.

CHOCOLATE CUPCAKES

Ingredients

For a 12-hole cupcake pan

7 oz / 200 g bittersweet (plain) chocolate (70% cocoa solids)

Scant ½ cup / 100 g butter

¾–1 cup / 200 ml milk

1 egg

⅓–½ cup / 100 ml sour cream

½ cup / 100 g sugar

2½ cups / 250 g all-purpose (plain) flour

2 tsp. cornstarch (cornflour)

1 tbsp. baking powder

1 pinch salt

Method

Prep and cook time: 50 min

1 Pre-heat the oven to 350°F (180°C / Gas Mark 4).

2 Chop the chocolate into small pieces. Melt the butter in a pan. Whisk the milk, egg, sour cream and sugar using an electric mixer. Place the flour, cornstarch, baking powder and salt in a bowl and mix until combined. Now pour in the milk–egg mixture, the melted butter and the chocolate pieces and stir until smooth.

3 Place a paper baking cup into each hole of the cupcake pan and pour in the cake batter, just about filling each cup. Bake on the middle shelf of the oven for about 30 minutes. Let cool in the cupcake tin for 10 minutes, then remove and place on a wire rack to cool completely.

DOUBLE CHOCOLATE CHIP COOKIES

Ingredients

Scant ½ cup / 100 g soft butter

¼ cup / 50 g sugar

½ cup / 100 g brown sugar

1 large egg, beaten

1 tsp. vanilla extract

1¾ cups / 170 g all-purpose (plain) flour

3 tbsp. cocoa powder

1 tsp. baking powder

¾–1 cup / 150 g chocolate chips (70% cocoa solids)

Method

Prep and cook time: 40 min

1 Preheat the oven to 350°F (180°C / Gas Mark 4). Line a cookie sheet with baking parchment.

2 Cream the butter with the sugar and brown sugar until light and fluffy. Gradually beat in the egg and the vanilla extract. Mix the flour, cocoa powder and baking powder and carefully stir in.

3 Fold in the chocolate chips. Put teaspoonfuls of the mixture in heaps on the cookie sheet, leaving about 2 inches (5 cm) between them. Place in the oven and bake for 10–12 minutes.

4 Let cool on the cookie sheet for 5 minutes, then take off and cool on a cake rack.

Published by Transatlantic Press

First published in 2010

Transatlantic Press
38 Copthorne Road, Croxley Green, Hertfordshire WD3 4AQ

© Transatlantic Press

Images and Recipes by StockFood © The Food Image Agency

Recipes selected by Jonnie Léger, StockFood

A catalogue record for this book is available from the British Library.

ISBN 978-1-908533-53-1

Printed in China